A DIAMOND IN THE ROUGH

FINDING A DIAMOND IN THE MIDST OF ALL THE OBSTACLES CAN BE DIFFICULT, BUT WHEN YOU DO FIND IT, THE BEAUTY REALLY STANDS OUT.... ARE YOU A DIAMOND WAITING TO BE REVEALED? LET US FIND THOSE DIAMONDS THAT HAVE BEEN HIDING FOR SO LONG....

TABLE OF CONTENTS

Dedication

Introduction

Chapter 1: Hidden

    A. Chosen and Called

Chapter 2: Buried

    A. Under the surface

    B. Invisible

Chapter 3: Exposed

    A. Uncovered

    B. Stir up the Gift

Chapter 4: The Assignment (Purpose) Revealed

    A. Details

B. Blueprint

Chapter 5: Procrastination

   A. Fear of the Unknown

   B. Avoidance

Chapter 6: Awakening

   A. Intense Heat

   B. Burning Within

Chapter 7: The Process

   A. Trials

   B. Loss of strength

Chapter 8: Pruning

   A. Separation

   B. Cutting

   C. Isolation

D. Waiting

Chapter 9: Pressure

    A. Intensity

    B. Pushing

Chapter 10: Revealing the Diamond

    A. Rise to the Surface

    B. Awareness

    C. Acceptance

    D. The Reveal

Chapter 11: A Diamond in the Rough

    A. How it all began

    B. Tried in the Fire

    C. Called to Serve

    D. Knowing Your Worth

The Dedication

This book is dedicated in the memory of my mother, Bettie W. Smith, who always made me feel like a rare jewel by the way she nurtured and loved me. Because of her exemplary lifestyle and her constantly showing me through her struggles how to weather the storms of life I am the woman I am today. There will never be a woman like her to ever walk this earth. I have the courage and ambition to pursue my dreams because of her prayers, love, and dedication to always supporting her children in whatever we chose to do. Although I am sure I disappointed her many times she always encouraged me to keep getting back up and not give up. Most of all she taught me to be a woman of God and how to trust and believe God no matter how bad your situation may be.

This book is also dedicated to my father, James I. Smith Sr., who recently left this earth to receive his eternal reward. You were always my hero and my protector. I learned so many valuable lessons from you throughout my lifetime. I will always cherish all the memories and moments we had together. Although my heart is broken and still hurting from the loss of you, I am determined to continue to make you proud of me. I love you daddy. Rest in Heaven.

This book is also dedicated to my husband and love of my life, Pastor Dennis R. Williams, Sr. I am so glad that God allowed you to find me and ask me to be your wife. Our life together has been an amazing journey, and I am looking forward to our continued future together. You are such an inspiration to me of how God can use a little boy at an early age to win souls to Him and continue to have that same fire in you to continue to win souls even into adulthood. You inspire me to keep going no matter what. We have been through many ups and downs, but we continue to build love and respect for each other after every obstacle we face. We are not perfect, but we are perfect for each other. I love you with all my heart and I pray this book will bless your life.

Lastly, I dedicate this book to my abusers, backstabbers, haters, naysayers, and enemies. You are the fuel that lights the fire that burns within. Because what you meant for evil God turned into his Glory!!!

Introduction

We are about to embark on a journey that will take you to a place that many of us do not wish to enter. Where is this place, you may ask? Well let me answer that question for you, it is in that hidden place that we carefully guard to prevent others from seeing our weaknesses, vulnerabilities, and shortcomings. But the time has come for you to be revealed and no longer hidden. I am aware that this will not be an easy task. I know because I am also taking this journey with you. In the world that we live in there are so many people who need to hear your story, who need to feel like they can get back up again, and that their situation does not have to be a fatal one. This seems so easy to say but not as easy to accomplish. The reason is we do not want to go through the process of being revealed. When a person is revealed, it can make you feel exposed. So, what do you do, hide again because facing the truth can mean admitting to others that you are not as perfect as you have portrayed yourself to be? Guess what? Most people already knew you were just behind a mask. Whether or not we realize it or not we communicate who we are and reveal a lot about ourselves not just verbally but also nonverbally. Hiding is a natural protective mechanism that just naturally happens when we are afraid of something or someone. We use it to protect us from hurt or harm. So why should we reveal ourselves, you might ask? Well simply because someone's life depends on it. The treasure on the inside needs to come forth so that it can bless someone who has long awaited that blessing. Will you come forth or remain hidden?

I am sure you have heard the phrase "a diamond in the rough." What do you think this phrase might mean? Let us explore this topic by giving you an example. In the movie Aladdin, the character Jaffar is in search of a diamond in the rough to enter a cave to retrieve a treasure he is in search of. This person must be one with a pure heart. It did not mean that he was perfect because in the movie, Aladdin was later revealed as the person who was the diamond in the rough. Aladdin was considered a street rat, a thief, and a nobody. Jaffar was shocked that someone of such low esteem would be the diamond in the rough. Aladdin retrieves the lamp and was given three wishes. His first wish is to be a prince(mask) because that is what he sees as his way to marry the princess. But in the end, all he had to do was just be himself instead of being someone he pretended to be to impress others. The moral of this story is that he was already a diamond, but it took many trials, challenging times, attacks from the enemy and death before he realized who he really was. How does this apply to real life? Regardless of how others may see you or what they say you are, you need to know that if your heart is pure eventually that type of heart will reveal the diamond that you are.

So, what is the process of forming a diamond? Since we have established that the gem(diamond) is hidden, what is the process of revealing the diamond? We will explore these steps in greater detail as we move forward. Step one in revealing the diamond is a deep burial in the earth's crust. Step two is to apply very intense heat. Step three is to apply intense pressure. Finally, step four is to rise to the surface. The process is not easy, but it is necessary.

My process of revealing the diamond in me is a hard and tedious journey that at times I did not want to go through. When I was born, I was a premature baby and only weighed 4lbs 11oz. Even then God had his hand on my life. I did not have to be in the incubator because the doctor said I was strong and did not need it. I did have problems with my lungs and dealt with asthma for the next 8 years. I never thought there was anything special about me as a child except unconditionally loved by my parents. When I started school at age 4, I realized the world did not love me unconditionally. I was very shy and quiet, so I became the target of bullying early. My mom had to come to the school at times to manage issues. At age 8 we moved to another city in the middle of my third-grade year. It was at this point that I met a teacher who would change my life. I was put in her class because my reading scores were lower, but she never made me feel less than any other student. She often encouraged me that I could do anything and not to let what others think stop me. Her words have been imprinted in my mind even until today. My mom was a devout Christian and we attended church regularly from the time I was born. My mom's life that she lived introduced me to Christ. She was always praying and helping others in need although she had seven children to take care of, she still cared for others as well. It taught me to care for others and it is the reason I chose to become a nurse. We were a simple middle-class family just like any other, but I struggled even then with self-image, self-worth, and self-esteem. I did not even know the meaning of those words then but as I look through the mirror of my past, I can see the struggle started early. As the years went on and I got older I started receiving attention from boys and even men about how pretty I was. At the time it made me feel good to hear it because my mom and dad often said it. But I was unable to distinguish the motive behind the words. Later in life those words would bring fear. Why? Because the words preceded a behavior that was inappropriate. It started with inappropriate touching and then escalated to attempted rape at 11 and rape at age 16 and 18. I never reported any of them because of fear of being ridiculed or blamed. I watched it happen to other girls who reported it. Today I look back and see clearly that I should have reported it because it could have prevented them from doing it to someone else. My life has been filled with pain, hurt, and disappointment. There are so many more incidents that I could tell but I am going to focus on the healing part. My process, I believe, began when I had my oldest son at age 19. Through many obstacles I persevered but I had not dealt with the pain of my past. I saw myself as damaged not a diamond. The diamond was hidden deep inside of me but only God could reveal it. At the age of

20 I gave my life to Christ and dedicated myself to serving him and others. Today I have been married for 28 years and I have three children. I am a nurse, and I am a life mentor. My process is still ongoing, but I am using my experience to bring healing and wholeness to other women who have been through similar situations. God did the healing, and I am liberated but I still have struggles even now, but the difference is I know my worth and I do not allow anything or anyone to disturb my peace.

So, let us travel on this journey together to reveal what is hidden in you and bring it forth…

Chapter 1

Hidden

If you were to go to try and find a diamond, it would take you to a place deep into the crust of the earth, with the right conditions to reveal what we know today as a diamond. So how do we go about revealing the diamond that is you? Well, many years ago when you were formed in your mother's womb gifts were placed in you that would only be revealed at the right time with the right conditions. You may be thinking exactly what the right conditions, or the right time is going to be for you. Well, that will depend totally on God's timing. The process could take years of preparation and the use of the right tools needed to bring forth the diamond. While you may use tools used to get deep enough to produce the diamond or bring it to the surface, there are not natural tools used to bring the diamond that is you forward. Let us look at the process of revealing the diamond. It may take pain to start your process. Your process may begin at birth with your parents giving you up for adoption. Yet someone else's process may start with years of abuse at the hands of those you expect to protect you. Or you began your process by being the victim of incest or molestation. But however, your process begins, there is an appointed time for the diamond to be revealed. Even others may say I had a great start to my life. They may say I grew up in a well to do family and I was always able to get whatever I wanted so I am already a diamond but are you really? Just because you did not experience abuse, incest, molestation, or rejection does not mean that you are automatically a diamond because you have access to the finer things in life. Society has programmed us to think that we are somebody by how much money we make, what we drive or where we live. However, it does not matter about any of those things because each of us has a purpose and plan for being born. We do not have control of how, when, where and to whom we are born. But what we do have control of, is how we use what we were born with. Each of us has a purpose for being here but it is up to us to walk in it. I am sure many of you are familiar with the story of Aladdin. He felt like he was a nobody. He ran the streets stealing for a living without a care and without purpose, so he thought. Do not ever think that your life has no purpose. Trust me my friends and believe that you would no longer be on this earth if your life did not have a purpose. But back to Aladdin. He did not realize that he was truly a diamond in the rough. He feared the truth about who he really was and so he pretended to be someone else to impress a girl he wanted. How many times do we become trapped in the world's ideology of what we should be, how we should talk, what we should look like or what success looks like. Aladdin thought the princess wanted a prince when all she wanted was someone who was true to who they were. She experienced the true Aladdin when he helped her in the market and when he revealed finally that he was not a prince but just a homeless boy trying to survive the life that had come his way. The girl in this story looked beyond what she could see on the outside and focused on the heart and love of others that was hidden on the inside. So, when a gift is placed on the inside of you, it may take tragic circumstances to reveal the gift, but it will eventually come forth. In Aladdin's case it took a near death experience for him to realize he should tell the truth and deal with the consequences. Instead, though he continues in the lie until it is later revealed. This story ends positively with him marrying a princess, but it could have ended tragically. Revealing the diamond is never a painless process because frequently we do not realize that we are a diamond until we are put into situations that show us who we really are. But once you know who you are you must take caution not to become arrogant with what you have been blessed with. We sometimes use the treasure on the inside for our own benefit. Whatever was placed on the inside of you was not for you but for others. When we focus on the purpose of the diamond being revealed then we understand that it is precious and yet it was revealed in you to show others what they can become. Like Aladdin in this example, I have found myself in the same position. I have always known that I was called to do a work for God but on the inside, I did not feel like I was good enough to be used by God. For a long time, I allowed my current state to determine what I could do. God had to remind me that I cannot do anything without His help. I had to learn to lean and depend totally on Him for my strength. I did not realize for a while that I had a treasure on the inside that I was not allowing to come forth because of fear. When you know that you have gifts and a calling on your life to work for God, you cannot let anything stop you from fulfilling it, especially fear. Fear can be paralyzing and bring everything to a standstill. In the story of Aladdin, he decided to take a step forward and go into the cave to retrieve the lamp and his life changed dramatically because he took the first step in faith. As for me, I decided that I was not going to allow my fears or flaws stop me from walking fully in my calling and using the gifts that God blessed me with to bless others. So, I took a leap into the unknown and my life has never been the same.

Chosen and Called

In the story of Aladdin, the evil villain Jaffar recognizes that Aladdin is the diamond in the rough he needs to obtain a treasure he so desperately wants. Just like Aladdin many of you have hidden gifts and callings that you may not be aware of. We are not always aware that we have been chosen for a specific path. The path that you will travel was chosen even before you were born. Your treasure on the inside of will remain hidden until the time appointed for you to come forth. Matthew 22:14 says "For many are called, but few are chosen." If you have been chosen, you should count it an honor. There will only be a few who will be chosen but as you will soon find out it will not be easy. In our story Aladdin soon finds out that being chosen for the task that was given to him almost cost him his life. Many of us that will be chosen or have been chosen soon to find out that there is a price to pay to be chosen. At the beginning I talked about the process of revealing a diamond. The process of revealing it requires you to go deep down to try to find it. Even after the diamond is found, it has not been revealed. It was in the dirt and under all the elements found in the earth's crust. So, to reveal what we know as a diamond there is a process. Let us go back to Aladdin. His true worth was hidden under the life that he was living as a homeless person stealing to survive. On the surface it would seem as if this would be the last person to be considered a diamond in the rough. As the story continues it reveals that it was not about his outer appearance, his socioeconomic status or even his lifestyle. It was, however, about his heart. He was chosen because his heart was pure. Regardless of what life has shaped you to be because of your environment, influences, or circumstances beyond your control you have been chosen. Let us understand about being called. Many will be called to different areas of life. This is the reason we have people working in all different vocations and careers because that is where they have been called. But when you happen to meet the rare few that have been chosen you find out the difference. What is the difference, you may ask? The difference is the chosen approach their calling as if they were born to do it. Why? Because when you realize you have been chosen, and you know your worth and your purpose is planned. Your entire life from this point on will be changed according to your chosen purpose. As I am sure you are aware, this is not an effortless process. Just like the process in revealing the diamond or Aladdin becoming a Prince, the preparation can be hard, tedious, and difficult. The results of this process are worth it but come journey with me as we navigate our way to revealing the diamond in the rough.

CHAPTER 2

Buried

When you think about something being buried usually what comes to mind is someone being put six feet under dirt and a tombstone on top. But that is not always the case when I think of being buried. Let us look at the diamond again. When the diamond was originally buried, it was buried far below the earth's crust. This indicates that it was much farther than six feet under. Also, another example can be a mental burial. So many people bury pain, hurt, trauma, depression, and many other things that they want to try not to face or think about. You see we feel like when something is buried it is final. But as you know life, people, and circumstances have a way of digging up what has been buried.

Under the Surface

When things are buried under the surface there are processes taking place while there. What may you ask? Well, when a person is buried six feet under it usually means they have died, had a funeral, and was buried. But while they are buried the decaying process progresses the longer the body is there until eventually all that will be left is bones. Unless there is a request for the body to be exhumed for DNA or evidence of a crime then the process will not be interrupted. But in the case of the diamond, staying buried under the surface will prevent those who seek the treasure from finding it. So therefore, many people search for, dig up and discover diamonds and they no longer remain under the surface. Just as the diamond will not remain under the surface neither will the many different things people bury in their subconscious mind. We may desire for it to remain under the surface, but life will not allow it. In the case of you and me, mental burial is a coping mechanism for what you experienced in that moment. Our body has a natural way of burying things to protect us from traumatic experiences. But naturally if these things are not dealt with, they will emerge from under the surface and manifest in our everyday life. When you have a mental burial, it must be dug up so that it can be dealt with, and healing can take place. You may want to forget about it and pretend like it did not happen, but you cannot. When something or someone triggers that memory, it resurfaces and can cause more trauma. It is particularly important to heal and not bury for this reason. Burying only means that it is out of sight for the moment, but it can resurface if not dealt with. I am speaking to you from experience. I stuffed things inside and buried them for years only for them to resurface and manifest in bad choices and destructive lifestyle and more trauma. Dealing with the things that have been buried on the inside can save you from years of destructive and irrational behavior. Do not allow anything that will affect your life eventually to remain buried. Let it emerge to the surface and deal with it.

Invisible

To be invisible means that you cannot be seen by the human eye. But we are going to approach this in a unique way. When you are in a room full of people all around you, but you feel invisible what does that mean? When you do not fit in with a certain group you may appear invisible to that group because they do not recognize you on their level. Let us revisit the story of Aladdin. He was considered by society as a nobody. He was called a "street rat"! To the people he was invisible because he was considered beneath them. When a person is physically buried, they can be considered invisible because they will never be seen again. But when feelings, hurt, etc. are buried we often feel invisible. Because we are hiding things on the inside, you feel like they are invisible because others cannot see them and therefore you function as if they are invisible. But life has a way of bringing the buried, under the surface and invisible things to light for all to see. Aladdin was seen when he was changed into a prince and had worldly possessions that caused people to see the one who was treated as invisible. What about you? What is on the inside of you may not be visible to us now but eventually it will become visible. Do not allow your past to hurt and remain invisible and under the surface. If you do not bring them to the light to be dealt with, you will carry them into your future. Keeping things invisible stunts our growth and only allows others to see the person you pretend to be. Do not let the circle force the invisible things to come forth but bring them forth on your own so that healing and wholeness can take place. When Aladdin was invisible, he was authentic. As soon as he tried to be someone else, he was a fraud. He had to bring forth the truth so that who he truly was could come to the surface. As the story progressed, he realized that he was always visible to those who viewed him with their heart. As for you, the façade that you are portraying while hiding who you are is not invisible. Those of us who see you with truth in our hearts can see the real you. So, stop burying the invisible things and bring forth your truth. Being your authentic self tells God that I am available just as I am, and I am ready to be used by you. God cannot use you while you are pretending to be someone you are not. You should not be ashamed of the person God made you to be. God used our experiences and our past to shape us into a vessel to be used by him. It is all about going through the process of becoming who you are called to be. Do not fight the process!!

CHAPTER 3

Exposed

When we think of the word exposed there are many things, I am sure that will come to your mind. Let us explore some of them. To be exposed means to be uncovered, unprotected, vulnerable, defenseless, and unsheltered. Any of these phrases describe what being exposed truly means. For further exploring I want to emphasize that when a person is exposed it is a place where they are the most vulnerable. Think about the times where you did something in secret, and it was exposed. How did it make you feel? I am sure you felt like you were naked and not covered. As we journey through this life, we will find out that we will be exposed at some point in our lives. Being exposed is not necessarily a dreadful thing all the time. Many times, for instance we have talents that we have kept hidden, and it takes the right circumstances to expose what we knew was down on the inside of us all along. Exposure can open the door for greater opportunities and possibilities in your life. If your gifts had not been exposed, where would some of you be today? I recall the first time I heard Bishop TD Jakes it was at Bishop Carlton Pearson's Azusa Conference. God used Bishop Carlton Pearson to expose the gift of Bishop TD Jakes to the world. After this exposure came years and years of ministry that has changed the lives of countless people. I know that exposure is not always easy, but it is necessary for God to get us through our process.

Uncovered

Now that we have established what uncovered means, let us find an example from our story Aladdin. Aladdin becomes a prince from a wish he made, his identity is uncovered by an evil villain named Jafar. It is then his identity is revealed. How many times have we been wearing masks pretending to have it all together, pretending to be knowledgeable about something or simply trying to impress someone important only to be exposed when the truth is uncovered. Why is it that we as human beings feel like we must pretend to be recognized by others that we are somebody? One reason may stem from our past. What type of environment did you grow up in? Were you rich or poor? Did you have a lot of friends or were you a loner? There are so many questions we could ask that would eventually uncover your true reason for wearing a mask or being someone, you are not. People who wear masks or pretend are doing it sometimes to protect themselves from hurt and pain. Others do it out of fear of how they will appear to society or the ridicule that may come. Sometimes all people want is to see the real authentic you. Flashback to our story when Aladdin was uncovered and his identity was revealed, he continued to lie to cover himself. But what he failed to realize is that Jasmine did not care that he was a prince. She fell in love with the person

Aladdin not Prince Ali. As for us, we must be ok with the person God made and present our true authentic self to the world regardless of the response. If you lose an opportunity by being truthful, it simply means there is another opportunity that is for you. You do not have to wear a mask or pretend just to be liked or accepted. It does not matter what people say about you, it only matters what God knows about you. Remember God loves us unconditionally. He knows all our flaws and he still love us and gives us grace, mercy, and favor. So, do not walk around wearing masks or pretending because eventually you will be uncovered and how will you respond?

Stir-up the Gift

After you have been uncovered what are you going to do? Will you keep lying to cover the lies you have already told? Will you just choose to be who you really are and allow the world to see you? If you choose to continue lying it will only lead to destruction. Nothing good ever comes out of a lie. The truth may be difficult to bring out and uncomfortable to reveal but it is necessary. If you are going to go forward, you must embrace who you are and what is in the inside of you waiting to come out. It is time to stir up the gift that has been lying dormant your entire life because of a mask.

When you make the decision to be the person you were created to be there will be opposition. You may lose friends and family in this process but being who God created you to be is much more meaningful. God will always bring people in your life to help you on your journey. Sometimes you must be separated from others who are not included in God's plan for your life. But what you must remember is that you already have in you everything you need to accomplish your purpose and goals. Stirring up the gift will require focus, skill, knowledge, and most of all wisdom. Your focus will become sharpened when the mask is moved but it is not completely clear because the mask has been on for a long time. How do I help my vision become clearer? First, I set my goals by writing them down. I make my goals plain and set a timeline to reach them. Second, I acquire whatever skills I need to obtain my goal. That may require training, research, and hard work. Third, I will gain the knowledge I will need to maintain my goal. It may require higher education, a mentor, or professional help. Last, when I have reached this point, I must be wise to know how to put to practice what I have learned so that I will be effective. These steps may seem basic but what you do not realize is that it may take numerous years to obtain. Everything that you do must be done with the right mindset or you will find yourself stuck in one place trying to get to your goal. Once the gift has been stirred it must be cultivated to be ready for use. If you have spent years living behind a mask or pretending it will not be changed in one day. There is a process for anything to grow so trust the process until it is complete. Growth requires time and effort to develop into the gift. You are not called one day and mature the next day. This may take many years before you are ready. God is using this time to develop your character and to make sure he can trust you with the gift. Do not rush the process because that can lead to disaster if you move before you are ready.

CHAPTER 4

The Assignment (Purpose) Revealed

Now that you have discovered the gift or gifts that are on the inside of you and taken steps to nourish and grow, it is time for your assignment. What do I mean by assignment? Well, it means you are about to be given something to do that will require the gift that has been revealed. When you were born your assignment was already written and ready, but you were not ready to receive it. Everyone born on this earth has a purpose for being born. Once your purpose has been fulfilled you will die. The fact that you are still living means your purpose is not completed. Purpose simply means the reason you were created. (Jeremiah 1:5)

When you were given an assignment in school what did you do? Most people who want to complete a successful assignment will start planning how to complete the assignment. They will start with doing research to gain knowledge on the subject. After the research has been done you may organize it and decide what you need for your specific assignment and eliminate what you do not need. A rough draft is completed first so that you can identify any mistakes or corrections that may be needed. Finally, you complete the final draft and turn it in to the teacher who grades your assignment. Sometimes you may receive an excellent grade and other times a bad one. But you never give up on improving your grade. So, with a spiritual assignment you start by receiving what

God has asked you to do and you seek his direction for your plan. When the plan is revealed, God sometimes allows you to go through trials and tribulations to prepare you for your purpose. This is like doing research on a paper. The research you are doing comes from the lessons you learn from your trials. You may fail to learn the lesson and must go through the trials more than once. During this process God is also developing your character for you to be prepared for your assignment. Unlike doing a simple research paper, your preparation time may be increased or decreased depending on you. It can be increased due to detours that we take after it has been revealed what we are called to do. Why do some people accomplish their assignment quicker while others take years? Well, it can be as simple as they prepared, did the work, and therefore they were successful in completing the assignment. But for others, they get prepared but somewhere along the way obstacles and distractions come and halt the progress. The assignment is completed but not in a timely manner. Completion of your assignment depends on your participation and God's timing. God gives us freewill to make our own choices. It is up to you to stay focused on your assignment and not be distracted by the devices of the devil. When we have an assignment from God, we must make it a priority. If you fail to make your assignment a priority, then you are open to whatever the enemy throws your way to detour from your assignment. Remember the devil comes to steal, kill, and destroy. Do not allow him to destroy what God has given you to do. Stay Focused!

Details

When God has given you an assignment the details are not always revealed all at once. In a natural assignment usually, you receive the assignment with all the details of what is expected for the assignment. With a spiritual assignment it may start with an idea that comes to your mind. The idea is sometimes dismissed and not addressed immediately. Then one day it returns to your mind again and you start to pray about what you have been given. For instance, I was given an idea to start a group to encourage other women who have been or are going through situations that I have encountered in my lifetime. I had an urgency to complete this assignment. When the thought initially came, I acknowledged that it was a great idea and that I should do it, but I put it off. Life got busy and although I kept thinking about it, I did not do anything. The first thing we must do when God gives us an assignment is first seek him for direction, then obey him. In Genesis 12:1, it says "Now [in Haran] the LORD had said to Abram, "Go away from your country, and from your relatives and from your father's house to the land which I will show you;" Genesis 12:1 AMP. Abraham has been given an assignment to leave everything and everyone that is familiar and go to a place where God is going to show him. To complete this assignment Abraham had to listen to what he was asked to do then obey. He had to take the first step and then he was leading every step of the way as long as he obeyed God. In my case. I heard God and he gave me instructions what to do but I did not obey then. After several months of putting it off, and several things going wrong in my life, I was presented again with the assignment. This time the urgency to obey was so strong that I heard God say, "Do it today!!" I got on my computer, and I just started doing as God led me to do and today, I have a women's ministry that reaches many women and have inspired and is bringing healing and restoration. When God gives you an assignment, he may not give all the details, but when you take a step-in obedience, he will reveal the details for each assignment he gives. God does not reveal an assignment in the same way with everyone so be prepared to receive it however he chooses to reveal it to you. Staying prayerful and spiritually alert helps you to be in place and ready to receive what God wants you to do. Establishing a consistent prayer life connects you to God and builds a relationship. When you pray you are communicating with God. You are talking to him, but he also talks to you and reveals his will to you through prayer. This is essential for being open to hear from God.

Blueprint

Usually when you think about a blueprint, you think about a written plan on paper. A blueprint according to the dictionary is a designed plan or other technical drawing. It also means to draw up (a plan or model). So why would you need a blueprint with an assignment? Let us explore this. In the word of God, it says "Then the LORD answered me and said, "Write the vision and engrave it plainly on [clay] tablets So that the one who reads it will run." Habakkuk 2:2 AMP. So, when we are given a vision(assignment), we should write it down. Writing down your plans brings life to it because you not only have a vision, but you now have plans on how to bring the vision to reality. Some blueprints can be hard to understand but we must remember to be specific in our plans. It is hard to complete any assignment without having the right amount plans. If you have a blueprint for your home, it details where each room will be located, how large and wide they will be and whether it is a bedroom, living room, kitchen, bathroom, etc. The architect draws the design to give the builder a map on how to build. You have been given an assignment and God has given you his blueprint which is the Bible. In the Bible, it gives you specific directions on anything you need to know to complete your assignment. If you follow the directions, you will complete your assignment. The problem comes when you turn away from your blueprint and try to do it on your own. It may work and even be successful, but it will not last. It is always better to obey than to sacrifice. When you make a choice, you are also choosing the consequences. Follow the blueprint and find peace and joy on your journey.

CHAPTER 5

Procrastination

On this journey we call life we will face many things that become obstacles to you walking fully in your purpose. One of the greatest obstacles I have found during my lifetime is procrastination. Simply put procrastination is just putting things off for another time. Procrastination has been the cause of failed businesses, marriages, relationships, careers, and the list goes on. Putting things off until later can lead to days, months and even years. There are some instances where procrastination may work to your advantage but usually it will not. We are going to explore two reasons why many find themselves procrastinating.

Fear of the Unknown

Fear can leave us paralyzed where we cannot move and therefore leave us vulnerable to the enemy destroying us. Fear of the unknown has caused many to not pursue their dreams and reach their goals. Let us just take Abraham as an example. What if fear of the unknown was stronger in his mind than the voice of God telling him to go. He did not know where God was sending him, but he trusted him and went. He would have missed the promise and the blessings because of fear. You may have found yourself in a situation where fear took over and you were hesitant to move forward. If you have not, I know I have found myself in this position. It takes time to overcome fear. Some people move past fear by deciding they will not allow it to stop them from reaching their goals. But others must battle with the thoughts and emotions of what could happen. Fear is a part of our life, but we do not have to allow it to control us so that we remain stunted. Do not get stuck in the same place and never step out and do what you have been called to do, do it afraid!! Remember God gave you the blueprint and he even took fear into consideration because he knows more about you than you know about yourself. Choose to have faith in God who has been with you every step of the way. His love drives out and starves fear. If you take a second and remember how much God loves you and accept that love, then you will not allow anything to stop you from your purpose. You have everything you need to overcome fear and go forth.

Avoidance

Being a procrastinator causes one to be an expert at avoidance. We think sometimes that if we avoid doing what we should do it will just go away. Things do not get better by being left alone. Problems do not get solved by avoiding dealing with them. Soon we find out that avoidance only prolongs the problem and does not solve it. In the story of Jonah, we see avoidance in its true form. He tries to avoid going to Nineveh and complete his assignment given by God so he gets on a ship thinking he can avoid doing what he was called to do. So fast forward he is thrown off the ship and swallowed by a gigantic fish prepared for him. After three days and nights in the belly he has a change of heart and obeys God and completes his assignment. So, avoidance can lead to consequences that will be unpleasant. Confronting your fears and not avoiding things can lead to a peaceful place where you can receive what God has for you while obeying his will. Those who have gone before you encountered fear and even tried to avoid what was in their heart to do but overcame it to walk out their purpose.

Procrastination is a way to keep you stagnant and unable to move forward. It will also cause you to not believe that if you were given an assignment that everything you need God has equipped you with to complete it. Do not settle for the menial when you have been called to do the mighty!! Polish that diamond who is you because you have been hidden long enough. It is time for you to stop procrastinating and obey what God has told you to do. The dream that you had, and you have yet to fulfill, it is time! Come forth!

CHAPTER 6

AWAKENING

When we think of an awakening, we think about waking up from sleep. But today our meaning of awakening simply means to become aware of something suddenly. We have been talking about our purpose and God revealing it to us. Now let us examine what happens when we are given a vision and some instructions of what to do but we have not been awakened to the fact that we have a call and an assignment because we are stuck in the procrastination phase. Let us use Paul for example. On the road to Damascus (Acts 9), Paul had an awakening experience with Jesus Christ and at that moment realized that he was being called to spread the Gospel. It may not take something as drastic for you to awaken to your assignment or to realize that you are a diamond (exquisite gem) chosen by God but for many it will. An awakening comes in different forms. It may be through the death of a loved one, a traumatic experience, a debilitating illness, and other things that God allows in our lives to awaken us to hear him. For me it took numerous things happening to me and around me to awaken me to the fact that I was chosen, and I must do what God called me to do. I was called by God to preach the Gospel at the age of twenty-seven and I started my assignment. My assignment changed four years later, and I rejected the assignment. So, for years I procrastinated and put off what God was calling me to do. But in 2007 my world as I knew it changed forever. I lost my mother. She was my best friend and most of all she was my prayer partner and spiritual mentor. This was truly an awakening for me because now my support system was taken from me, and I was grieving. There were two things that took place during the awakening process.

Intense Heat

First, intense heat is applied. For me it was going through the loss of my mother and all the emotions and stages of grief. It also was a time for me to find out who I really was without the help I was used to. When a diamond is being formed it must go through intense heat to burn off all the impurities that do not make the diamond authentic. As it is with us God allows things to come that will show us what we are made of and to mold us into what he wants us to be. Everyone goes through the heating process to be ready to shine like the diamond you are. The diamond could not really come forth until the heat was intensified to reveal the precious stone God created. The intensity of the heat is necessary to achieve the desired result. The heat is turned up to create something that is strong, resilient, and beautiful. When the heat is intense in your situation you may desire for God to remove you from the situation. But coming out of the fire prematurely can cause the diamond to not be as valuable as it should be or you to not be prepared for your assignment.

Burning Within

Secondly the awakening causes an inward burning which I called an urgency. This inward burning happens when you realize who you are in God, stop procrastinating, and step out on faith to do God's will. I just want you to understand that this process does not happen overnight. In my example previously of Paul, he had to obey what he was told to do. Even when he started preaching, he faced so many obstacles, ridicule, doubt, and hate. But he had a passion burning within that would not allow him to quit. When you are called to an assignment from God, he promised that he would never leave you or forsake you so you must trust him. The passion that is burning within to some is not enough. But remember just like a diamond must go through the process to finally shine, your process takes time. We cannot let our feelings or emotions block us from completing our assignment. Yes, you will not always want to do it but do not give up. The reward at the end of the process is a beautiful diamond and your reward is eternal peace and a heavenly home. "Let us not become weary in doing good, for at the proper time we will reap a harvest if we do not give up." Galatians 6:9 NIV

CHAPTER 7

The Process

The process involves every step it takes for you to complete your assignment. As in the diamond process it starts beneath the surface and there are several steps that take place before the diamond is revealed. The process in the mind of God began before you were born. You are chosen before you were formed in your mother's womb. There are vessels that never made it to birth either because of being aborted or dying in utero. If you made it to birth it simply means you have a purpose for being here. Each of us has a path that have been chosen for us by God. It is called his perfect will. But when we choose not to walk in God's perfect will, he sometimes allows a permissive will. But do not think that because he permits something that he is ok with it. He is not!! The process, however, of walking in your purpose depends entirely on you. We are given a choice when we come into the knowledge to choose our path in life. But know regardless of which path you choose your choice will never override God's will for your life. How might you ask? Well let us see.

Trials

Trials are what prepare us to complete our assignment. When trials come in your life, they are showing you really what you are made of. Trials bring out strength you did not know you had. There is a purpose for everything that you are going through. We do not always know the purpose so therefore we respond to trials like an enemy. We want to eliminate the trial so our life can go on. What we fail to realize is our trial is currently a part of our life. For example, when I experienced rape, I just wanted it to stop so I could be safe. God kept me safe during it, but I did not see a purpose for the pain, hurt, and violation I experienced. It was years later before I knew the purpose for the pain. Understand that you will not always know why you or why this, but there is a plan for your pain. Each trial adds something and may take something away. My trust in others was taken away from me through my trials and it took God's divine healing and love to restore that trust. Through my trials I have learned to love God, trust God, love myself and love others. But most of all my trials help me find the true authentic me. When others saw the outward me and decided I was not good enough, God hid me like the diamond beneath the surface and when the time was right, dug me up, burnt off the impurities, polished me and sent me forth to those who knew my value and appreciated it. You see your trials do not only make you strong but a rare stone whose value is priceless. Our trials come to take us to a place where God can use us for his glory. Being victorious over our trials shows our readiness to obey God's will.

Loss of Strength

During our process, our strength is sometimes lost. Although trials bring us out stronger, we often lose strength during the process. We must be realistic when we are going through our process and know that we have an enemy who is constantly looking for a way to destroy us. "Be sober [well balanced and self-disciplined], be always alert and cautious. That enemy of yours, the devil, prowls around like a roaring lion [fiercely hungry], seeking someone to devour." 1 Peter 5:8 AMP Although we are aware of this fact, we find ourselves losing ground. We let distractions creep in and cause us to lose focus. Whenever we take our focus off our purpose and what we have been called to do then we begin to lose strength and the enemy devours us through depression, anxiety, disappointment, stress and so many others. So how do you keep from losing your strength? I am glad you asked. The answer is simply put your total trust in God who is your main source of strength. You may be thinking I have a support system in place in case I need strength but remember they are human. People are not always available, but God is always with you and never leaves. Whenever I find myself needing strength I turn to prayer. It is a conversation with God that allows me to speak my truth to God along with how I feel about it. It is also a time for me to listen to him for guidance and direction. I never leave prayer without strength and encouragement. Try it because it works!! **Strength is also built through studying and meditating on the word of God. Whatever you are facing, God's word has a solution.** His Word says, "weeping may endure for a night, but joy comes in the morning" Psalms 30:5.

So you can be encouraged in knowing that your situation may be dark, and your strength may be small, but the morning is coming with joy!

CHAPTER 8

Pruning

So, when you think of pruning, you are thinking about trees. I know because I thought about that also until God revealed what pruning is in the spirit and not the natural. So, when God allows pruning to take place in your process of being revealed as the diamond you are it means he is removing the dead things so that you can grow. Let me give you an example of my pruning process. Because of my past hurts I had a problem with trust, I battled with self-esteem issues, self-worth, depression, and anxiety. In my pruning process God allowed people in my life who took the time to pray for me and help me to work through these issues. He also allowed situations to happen that cut off the source of most of these problems. Pruning is cutting off. I had to cut off relationships, ideologies, and how I saw things for growth to happen. When we stop seeing things through our eyes and start to see things through God's eyes our perspective changes. God helped me to realize who I was according to him not people. He also directed me to the only example I should live my life by and that was Jesus Christ who is the perfect example of how we should live our lives. I knew all of this from being raised in the church my entire life, but it is not the same when it becomes personal. My walk with Christ was being hindered by the things in my life that were taking over my mind. When I stopped and allowed him to renew my mindset then my actions followed. Instead of allowing my circumstances to overwhelm me, I used them to propel me to walk fully in my calling. The pruning process is a very intricate part of the process. So, let us explore the steps of pruning.

Separation

Pruning happens when you cut away the dead or unproductive part of trees or plants. In your life pruning happens when God begins to reveal to you the things, habits, and behaviors that you need to correct or let go of. As a Christian our job is to spread the Gospel to others so that they might receive Jesus Christ as their Lord and Savior. If there is anything in you that hinders that from happening, then it is time to prune. Let us just take for example a woman who has a goal to own her own business. She was abused as a child and she is in an abusive relationship that is mentally, physically, and emotionally abusive. Her road to reaching her goal will be an uphill battle. Her confidence is not there so in her case, pruning starts with someone who continues to reassure her that she is fearfully and wonderfully made. If you do not know who you are, it will be difficult to believe in yourself to accomplish anything. Also, she needs to know that through Christ she can do anything. It is important to know that you have some help on your journey. Understand that the separation part of pruning requires identifying areas that are not productive and dying. Sometimes separation requires the use of force to separate. In our example it may require leaving and seeking help. This is just your first step now let us move further.

Cutting

Once we have found and identified the dead and unproductive parts it is time to cut. The dying parts cannot be allowed to remain, or it will stunt the growth and no fruit will be produced. To be effective in the kingdom we must go through spiritual surgery. When you are called to complete an assignment there are certain things that must be cut out for healing and growth to happen. During surgery you are not allowed visitors in the operating room. This means we are separated from those who are not necessary for the cutting process. Then, before cutting, the area must be sterilized and clean from the inside and outside. On the inside you are not allowed to eat or drink after a certain time to prevent you from getting sick after surgery. On the other hand, on the outside the area must be cleaned to prevent infection once the cutting happens. In spiritual cleaning the inside requires repentance from sin and the hidden things that no one sees including releasing those things from your mind that may cause spiritual sickness. Outward cleaning requires us to behave in a way that God is pleased with, which means live the life you preach. We are to be an example of Christ as we are his disciples. During the cutting process, diseased, injured, or dying parts are cut and removed. Anything in you that should not be, will be removed, so that healing can begin.

New Growth

The last step in the pruning process is new growth. So now that those things that were holding you back have been found, cut, and removed, the healing process starts. I found out recently just how slow the healing process can be after surgery. But I also saw what God was doing spiritually as well. My journey began with me going back and forth to the doctor to find out the problem. A part of my body was not functioning as it was created to function, so we tried medication. Finally, we realized that the damaged part needed to be cut out for my body to function normally. So, since we were in a pandemic the process included several steps, including taking a COVID test and quarantining for one week prior to surgery. This meant I had to get off the job prior to surgery. Also, I had to stop taking certain medications and could not eat or drink after midnight prior to surgery. On the day of the surgery no one was allowed to go back with me. Surgery took place and I was sent home with instructions for the healing process. Now the healing process includes lots of rest, no lifting, and getting up some to move around to prevent blood clots. During new growth, we may be in pain, or be restricted on movement that allows time for rest to build our strength. Many times during this process, I became aware that I could not do everything I wanted to do because it was not time. Growth takes time and you cannot rush the process because you may have a setback and must slow down to heal properly. You may stumble or fall during the new growth, but God is there to pick you up and give you strength to keep going. God taught me to depend on and trust him during my process. Through my surgery and healing process I have seen God as provider, healer, miracle worker and my everything thing. Not only did my body heal, and experienced new growth, but I had growth in every area of my life. Pruning may sound like something that you would rather not deal with, but it is what must take place if you are going to walk in your purpose. You are hidden but God is about unveil the precious treasure that is you. He cannot do that until you have completed every step of your process. New growth means that there are opportunities that will be available because of you completing your steps.

Waiting

During the pruning process we also experience a period where we are waiting. God has us in a holding pattern. During this time, we often experience frustration. When God gives us an assignment, and we are going through the process of completing it, we expect it to be done in a timely manner. This, however, is not usually the case where God is concerned. The waiting period is the time God uses to make and mold you. He is building your endurance and patience. He knows that you will need this when you are fully walking in your calling. I did not understand this concept when I found myself in a holding pattern. I felt abandoned by God. During this season, people left my life that I thought would always be in my life. I thought I was experiencing a drought in my ministry, although I never ceased ministry. God removed people around me so that he could talk to me without the distractions around me. He started to drop ideas and visions in my spirit for my next assignment. This caused me to stay on my face before him for guidance and to seek direction in his word. I found myself with a greater hunger for knowledge to be more effective in ministry. God connected me to those who would give me spiritual guidance to the next level of my ministry. Also, in this season he revealed some things that I learned had to be unlearned and I was able to see the light of what he was showing me through his Word. I now understood that this waiting period was God's way of preparing me to complete my assignment. I began to understand that my assignment had changed. When God gives us an assignment, we must be aware that it will not be a lifetime assignment. It will change because he has more than one assignment for you. You may have originally been called to preach the gospel, but that assignment is not the only one. I found myself at a crossroad of my ministry and I had to adapt to this change during my time of waiting. This may sound so elementary because you may say It is just another assignment. Remember that each assignment comes with instructions, and you may be asked to do something that you are not comfortable doing. I was not comfortable in my waiting period. I asked God why many times while waiting. Waiting builds, but it also breaks down areas where you need help. You may be in a waiting period because he is building your character. You may be a person who has little patience. You may be someone with integrity issues and God needs you to walk in integrity. He must be able to trust us with our assignment, so we must go through our waiting period.

CHAPTER 9

Pressure

Pressure means to push against something using force. When pressure is applied, the object is forced to comply to the pressure because it is forced to do so. In our case pressure is allowed in our circumstances to force us to conform to the specific assignment we have been given. Without pressure we would go through life just getting by. When a deadline is given to you for an assignment you are forced to reach it or suffer consequences. This concept also applies to your spiritual assignment. If God does not allow pressure to be applied, we would procrastinate and complete the assignment when we felt like it. Pressure is a blessing because it keeps us focused on our tasks and helps to prevent detours along the way.

Intensity

Pressure as I mentioned requires force, but the intensity is different depending on what is required. When a diamond is being revealed it takes very intense pressure to reveal it. The process is tedious but necessary. Two years ago, God gave me an assignment by dropping the idea in my spirit. I immediately thought this is a wonderful idea and I will be doing what I love and helping others too. But then I did not act on it right away so I put it in the back of my mind thinking I will do it soon. Well soon turned into several months. At the end of the year in December I begin to get an urgency to do what God asked me to do. I could not sleep; things were happening around me that caused anxiety and I felt the pressure to go forth. But I did not do it until God spoke sternly to me one day in my living room and said, "Do it today!!" I got on my phone and just took a leap and started the ministry now known as Wonderfully Made Me. It took intense pressure to get me to stop procrastinating and do what God asked me to do. In the Bible 1 Samuel 16 records David being anointed as King of Israel. David did not immediately take the throne. He was tired from intense pressure. In 1 Samuel 17 David faces the giant Goliath. This was a test that was allowed to prepare David for his assignment as King. He defeats Goliath using a slingshot and a stone. What

God was trying to teach David was that you are going to face giants or problems that may be too much for you to manage but when you put your trust in God you can defeat any enemy. For others it may take losing someone or going through a terminal illness before you say yes, but whatever God must allow to bring you to a place where his will for your life is manifested, he will do. The intensity of the pressure applied takes us to the place where we walk in obedience to God. Since you will not go without the pressure, God increases the intensity through your trials. When a diamond is finally revealed it is strong. It has endured the process and is now ready to be used.

Pushing

Not only do you have intensity that adds to the pressure but pushing is a part of applying pressure. When I think of pushing, I think of someone who is standing still and is pushed forward to move you from a standstill. Completing your assignment will involve pushing at times. During the time that I was procrastinating doing what God had asked me to do, I had some intensity through trials, but a pushing is what caused me to act. In Genesis 22:2 in the Bible, God asks Abraham to sacrifice his son. This was Abraham being pushed to do something exceedingly difficult. Abraham obeyed God but then was instructed not to kill him. God's way of pushing in this instance was to evaluate Abraham's faith for God to provide a sacrifice. God needs to know that we can be trusted to carry out our assignment therefore he tests us or pushes us to show us how much we need him. If you find yourself at a pause from your purpose or assignment, you may just need a push to wake you up to move again. Regardless of what your assignment may be, it will require pushing to get you there. You must be able to take the intensity and the pushing, or you will not complete the assignment. Obstacles are going to come but remember you are more than a conqueror. You must even push yourself at times. I am a woman who enjoys encouraging others as well as helping people to heal, grow, and become whole. But there are times when I need a push, so I often encourage myself. Also, God knows when you need to be pushed so he sends others to push you, he allows storms to push you, and he even pushes you through speaking directly to you. There is no limit to pushing but whatever it takes to get your assignment completed.

CHAPTER 10

Revealing the Diamond

Now that you have gone through the process it is time to reveal the diamond. Each person will have a reveal that is unique to you. You are one of kind, so your reveal is especially designed for you. My personal reveal the first time came when I was called to preach. What we must be aware of is that your diamond has different facets meaning many parts, so all parts are not always revealed. I thought that when he revealed I was called to preach that I would be a missionary and work inside and outside the church telling others about Christ. But I would soon find out that the other facets had not been revealed. Everything in our life is about timing and only God knows the right timing for you. God sees our future where we can only see the present. If things are revealed to us before we are ready the outcome may not be favorable. I worked hard in the first facet. I did ministry right by my husband's side as a First Lady. During me doing what I thought God wanted me to do he revealed another facet. This time he revealed a prophetess. Initially I totally rejected that call because I was aware of the challenges that came with it. After spending time in prayer and asking God to forgive my rejection, I accepted my assignment. This facet took me through many years of challenges and growth in many areas of my life. Through my struggles I gained strength and courage to overcome. I learned more about me during this time and even revisited the pain and hurt of my past. This time my past hurts were used as steppingstones to push me forward. Also, during this time, I had to unlearn some things that had been holding me back from moving forward. God used this facet to polish me for the next facet. I suffered loss during this time, including my mother who was an extraordinarily strong presence in my life. Sometimes God will allow the props to be removed so we learn to lean on him. She was my prayer partner and my confidant. This loss took a great toll on me. I even questioned my faith, but God kept me through it. In every facet that is revealed there are lessons that we learn before he can reveal other parts. So fast forward 15 years before he revealed another facet. There is no time limit on how long you will be on an assignment. Time is for us because God deals with eternity. My next facet was revealed during one of the most difficult years of my life. There were struggles happening seemly in every area of my life. This time I started my assignment for the next facet right before this world was hit with a pandemic that would change life as we know it forever. I had no idea how to do it, but he has been my guide every step of the way. This time I am called a mentor. God is using my experiences to help others who are struggling in life. My struggles have not stopped but how I manage them has improved drastically. There are steps you will go through each time a facet is revealed in your diamond.

Rise to the Surface

The diamond is buried deep, and it must rise to the surface before it can be revealed. Our gifts and talents are hidden deep on the inside and to walk in our purpose those gifts must be revealed. To bring some things to the surface we must dig to retrieve them. On the other hand, when in the right environment or situation many times things just rise to the surface. The story of Ruth in the Bible shows us how circumstances push us to go places that lead us to what we are destined to do. She was a Moabite woman who were not supposed to have dealings with Jews and yet she marries one. After famine took away her husband, she is left with the choice to go back to her people or with her mother-in-law to a land where she was not welcome. She also chose to serve her mother in-law's God. On her path she found favor, married Boaz, and gave birth to the grandfather of David. She is named in a lineage of Jesus Christ. But she rose to the surface when her circumstances put her in position to rise. Unlike Ruth others must be dug up because their circumstances buried them so deep it takes a bulldozer to get them to the surface. This was the case for me. There was so much digging that had to be done for the true essence of who I was could be revealed. We individuals go through a tremendous amount of trauma, especially early in life and that comes with a lot of baggage. I spent years of my life stuffing things that happened to me and not talking about them. As a result of the stuffing, I developed trust issues along with bitterness, anger, shame and many more. There was a mountain of baggage to get through to reveal to me. But when God heals, he removes the baggage and through his word he tells me who I really am. With time complete healing took place to the point where I began to trust God and his plan for my life. Yes, it was a process, and it did not happen overnight but through prayer, counsel, and God's word I rose to the surface, and you can too.

Awareness

Getting to a place in life where a light bulb comes on in your head about your situation means you have become aware. Awareness enters our life when we connect with the one who is all-knowing and that is God. God reveals himself to us in several unusual ways. Each experience of true awareness is unique to everyone. Let us take Paul, in Acts 9 we are given the story of Saul who later became Paul awareness of who Jesus was and his authority. In this account Saul became aware of his own inadequacy compared to Jesus. A light shined on him so bright it knocked him off his beast. What it took for Paul's awareness may not be the same as yours, but each of us had our time. My awareness really came for me when I became a single mom at age 19. I knew that I had to change my life because now I had to raise a child and my example would be critical to that. I found myself at a fraternity party and no longer had any interest in being there. At the time I did not have a relationship with God personally, but I was raised in the church. I believe now that it was God speaking to me. The voice I heard said "Why are you here, you are a mother now!" I stopped dancing and left. After that I never attended another party. My awareness at this point was to be a better example of a mother. I am not saying you are not a good mother if you are partying, but I am saying to be ready for the consequences of your actions. My son saw me going to work, school and church as well as spending time with my family. I did not realize at the time that there was a greater assignment for me, but I know that this was the starting point for God getting me on track for what he would reveal in the future. Your awareness can happen at any stage of your life.

There is an appointed time for everyone. People are walking around feeling like they are aware but then God reveals a part that you were blind to until He was ready to reveal it. In Paul's case in Acts 9, he was blind until he obeyed what Jesus told him to do and then his eyes were opened. Each facet of me was revealed at various stages and I was not able to see it until I was ready to. Sometimes those of us on the outside looking in can see things in you but your awareness will come when God shows you.

Acceptance

In the world we live in acceptance is something we all want from the time we are born. An infant seeks acceptance from their parents when they cry and receive attention. We may view that as attention, but it is also acceptance of motherhood or fatherhood. As we grow, we search for acceptance from others such as extended family, friends, teachers, co-workers, pastors, and the list goes on. Although acceptance from others is good it should not consume your life. Instead, we should know we are accepted by God and all other acceptance does not even compare. God accepts us with all our flaws while others may reject us for the same reason. When God makes us aware of who we really are we automatically know that we are accepted. God's acceptance is shown through his love for us. God's love is unconditional. How do I know because he sent his son Jesus who did not know sin to die on the cross so that we could be saved and one day live in heaven? He suffered on our behalf when we did not deserve it. But his grace and mercy looked beyond our faults and accepted us into his family through the shed blood of Jesus. Now that is acceptance. There are those reading this who have been rejected by your parents, but you are still accepted by God. There is a place that you must get to where acceptance from others is not a goal, but to be pleasing to God. At this place you know that if God is pleased, acceptance from others does not matter. To complete God's purpose for your life, acceptance from others cannot be your priority. The world, meaning mankind will always fail you, and many will not accept you, but God accepts you just the way you are. There are times when acceptance is necessary, for instance getting into a college or getting a job. But even at these times, when we acknowledge God, he directs us to places we will be accepted. We are rejected at times when we fail to acknowledge God for the right path. Your choice may get you accepted, but at what cost? We must remember that we can only see to the corner, but God sees around the corner. We do not know the future, but God does. Acceptance requires us to put our total trust in God and not ourselves or the world's system. **Acceptance can also mean** receiving something. In this context of acceptance God is unveiling another facet of your diamond. He wants to get us to a place where we receive all that God has prepared for us. If you are going to be that diamond that he will reveal to the world, you must accept his love, his joy, his grace, his mercy, and his strength just to name a few. It takes all these assets to come forth. You are not aware of what you will face but you know his grace is sufficient for you. Receiving or acceptance from what God offers guides you through a path of success that no one can block. Acceptance is a vital step in your reveal.

The Reveal

Just as the process to revealing a Diamond is an incredibly detailed process, so it is when God reveals you. When a diamond is revealed, it is priced according to its appraised value. Therefore, you see several types of diamonds and different shapes. Each one of these diamonds is unique but valuable. Before you are revealed, God must allow you to be tried in the fire. While you remain in the fire your character is developing, gifts are coming to the surface, and you are learning who you truly are. During this transformation fear may set in and overwhelm you, but it is all a part of the process. The reveal has an appointed time. For God to reveal you and his purpose for you, preparation is a must. Being revealed prematurely before your time may cause you to take unnecessary detours and trials that would not have happened if you waited on God. Let us give an example. A young woman who wants to be a doctor goes to school, and gets a degree, and then goes to medical school for further training to become a doctor. The final part of her training is to do a residency program to get the direct training needed to become a doctor.

Now if this woman tries to operate on someone without the proper training it may cost someone their life. So, it is especially important to go through every step to be ready for what God has called you to do. Coming forth before you are ready may be detrimental to those to whom you have been called to. I want to encourage the person who has heard the call from God but stepped out prematurely before time. There is a process that each of us must endure to be everything that God has called us to be. Skipping the steps will only delay the process and may end up with you not completing your assignment. God calls each of us to a specific assignment. He has placed what you need to complete your assignment on the inside of you. But remember there is an appointed time and a process to get you to the final reveal. The process may be tedious, painful, and hard but it is necessary for the assignment. The reveal involves you being presented to others who may not love you like God does. You must be ready for the discouragement, the ridicule, and the rejection that will come with your assignment. Therefore, it is imperative to go through what it takes to prepare you for what is coming. God wants to reveal the diamond that has been hidden awaiting its unveiling and that diamond is "You." Ready or not here He comes!

Your Response

Now that you have been revealed, where do you go from here? This part of your life can be difficult.

God has brought you forth and revealed your purpose but many times we remain stuck. You know you have a calling, and you are aware of your purpose, but what comes next? Well, my friend It is time to launch into the deep. Jesus walked with his disciples while on the earth. He trained them and gave them instructions of what do, but they still felt inadequate to complete their assignments. We all go through the process of revealing, but we are often hesitant to really do what we have been called for. Jesus reminded his disciples that he would be leaving but he would send them a comforter to help. God has given us everything we need to complete our assignments, but we must be willing to use what we have learned from our process to be effective in our calling. You are now a diamond that has been brought to the surface and polished. You are ready to be used. Do not forget that a diamond requires maintenance to continue to shine. This means you must cultivate the gift that is being revealed. The reveal is just the beginning of you completing your assignment. This walk is done daily. We must continue what God started in each of us. You are a precious diamond, revealed by God, and fit for the kingdom. You are no longer hidden or a diamond in the rough, but you a simply a diamond. Now Shine!!

Chapter 11

A Diamond in the Rough

How it All Began

Let us take a step back and look at how it all began. This diamond that we will call Ivy, was born to two loving parents, but her process of emerging as a diamond has just begun. Ivy's childhood presented many challenges that would shape who she would become. This may be the story of this diamond but each of us has our own unique journey that we must travel to reach our purpose and destiny. Let us begin with Ivy who was born prematurely and had difficulties with her lungs and asthma as a child. She was an extremely sweet and shy little girl. She was loved and cared for in her home, but often bullied and mistreated outside her comfort zone. She managed to overcome several obstacles and adversities while attending school. Ivy met many role models that helped cultivate the teachings she learned from her parents. This little girl as it would seem has a good life. She has two loving parents and four siblings and a host of aunts, uncles, and cousins who were constantly a positive influence in her life. But as several of you can agree, everything is not always what it seems. Although her parents were always particular about who watched their children, there were things that took place even in the presence of trusted family and friends. This little girl's life changed drastically between the ages of 5-7. She became the victim of incest at the hands of three different family members. Her life would never be the same. Ivy began to become withdrawn, and she no longer had that same spark she once had. Ivy did not know how to manage the enormous number of emotions that flooded her mind. She did not know if she should tell her parents because her abuser had told her she would get in trouble if she did. So, Ivy began the process of stuffing things that happened to her due to being told not to tell anyone. After a few times she could not distinguish a good touch from a bad one. Every time she was in the presence of a boy or man, she became anxious wondering if she would be violated once again. These feelings led to Ivy having difficulty trusting others and building relationships. She felt like everyone wanted something from her. Her feelings eventually became reality as she grew older. This began a cycle of several types of abuse. She would experience attempted rape at age 11 by an adult in the church, as well as rape at the age of 16 and 18. This sent her mental state to a place where she could not recognize herself and was unable to talk about it to the ones who would have protected her. She had learned how to stuff her emotions and she did not know how to manage how these events made her feel. Trauma from abuse can and will affect every area of your life for the rest of your life unless you decide to seek help to heal. Healing may start with prayer to God, but it should also include professional therapy. What you have just read is only a portion of her story. You may see this as a familiar story or one you have heard too many times before. But remember that your story will follow you into your present and future. This story began simply with the innocence of a child but as you know that can change quickly and will change your mind and how you see and interact with others in the world. It matters how you start but that is not the end of your story. You do not have to be a victim of your story but a victor. You can overcome any challenges you may face but not alone. This young girl could not understand why the God she heard about at church would allow such dreadful things to happen to her. She began to feel resentment, anger, frustration, and bitterness. It does not matter how your story began because God is the author, and he knows what plans he has for you, and he will not put more on you than you can bear. For the diamond to be authentic and display its true value, it must go through the process.

Tried in the Fire

Being tried in the fire is necessary to get us to the place where we can be used by God. What does that look like in this young girl's life? Unfortunately, at an early age it is far from clear how any of the numerous challenges in your life will ever make sense. Let us explore that further. When trials and tribulations occur in your life, it has a purpose. Before we were formed in our mother's womb, God had a plan for you. For us to reach that place we must be tried in the fire. At the age of eighteen, Ivy found herself in a bad place in her mind. This would cause her to struggle with her self-esteem, her body image, and her self-worth. She also exhibited trust issues with people which led to building an internal wall to protect herself from hurt. Being tried in the fire means sometimes the heat is intense and that it puts us in a place of discomfort. God knows that we will need comfort and peace during these times. He will send people in your life to help you through this season. Just be mindful that some people are in your life for a season and not to stay. You must stay alert during this season because the enemy will also send people for your demise. Make sure you can distinguish between the two. When you are being tried you will have failures, disappointments, and mistakes that require you to go back through the process again. God's is molding and making you. The fire burns off anything that is not authentic. So be prepared to lose the masks, the walls, and everything that hides the authentic diamond God made you to be.

Called to Serve

Ivy's call to serve began when she gave her life to Christ at the age of twenty. She had not yet realized her true worth. The only thing she knew at this point was that she was a child of God. I know that most of you are thinking that should be enough. You are right but every child of God has a purpose and plan for their life that God preordained. When you receive Christ as your Lord and Savior you are excited and ready to serve. We are all called servants but to serve effectively we must be taught. God's word is our roadmap that guides us through life. God also sends us pastors after his heart to help us by preaching the gospel and directing us as he or she is directed by God. But Ivy realized that being called to serve came with tests and trials. She began developing a personal relationship with God in prayer and studying His word. It would eventually be revealed to her that she had a specific call on her life. Ivy, like many of us received a specific calling from God but she did not completely understand her assignment and how she would walk fully in it. When God gives you an assignment, it is the enemy's job to try to steal, kill, and destroy it. When you are not healed and you are dealing with unresolved trauma in your life, it can become a stumbling block to what God has in store for your life. Being called to serve is the highest honor anyone can receive from God, but never forget that there will be a price to pay as you serve. Ivy would soon realize as she walked through her journey of serving it would take her through more pain, disappointments, rejection, and questioning her self-worth.

Knowing Your Worth

Ivy found her life in turmoil too many times and she was struggling to manage it. As an adult she had worked for years and years serving God and immersing herself in ministry. She learned how to wear the different masks to please what she thought was God but, she was unaware that she was pleasing people and not God at all. As people of God, we can become so busy doing things that we feel are important to the ministry that we forget that we need to know who we are in God's eyes. God made us in his image and his likeness (Genesis 1:27), so we are unique in the eyes of God because we are like Him. God also told us that we are fearfully and wonderfully made (Psalms 139:14), therefore, we should believe who God says we are rather than mankind. But who are we kidding, we are human, and we want to fit in, be loved, and have status in society. Ivy found herself often trying to fit in where she really stood out. She did not know her self-worth. She became overwhelmed with the culture she found herself in and it was no longer satisfying. She began to have trouble sleeping and her stress increased dramatically due to life circumstances that brought back past trauma. Ivy found herself at a crossroad. She wondered should I just pray my way through this and allow God to heal me or do I go to a professional for help? This decision prompted her to talk to God in prayer as she had been taught. In the process of waiting on God for an answer she continued attending church and ministering to others who were experiencing hurt as well. Ivy was made aware through her personal encounters with God that she had been going through life doing what everyone wanted her to do and engaging in destructive behaviors because she never wanted to face what was wrong. She was not healed and whole, so her vision was blurred when it came to knowing who she truly was and what God required of her. If you do not know your worth you will think that you are inadequate to do what you are called to do. Ivy finally received her answer to the question she asked God, and it was do both. She opened the door for her healing and started going to therapy. It did not mean that she did not trust God to heal her, but she needed help from a professional and that was ok. For the first time in her life, she began to see her worth. How might you ask? She started to take care of herself and not just focusing on taking care of others. Taking care of yourself is not selfish but necessary to be effective in life and ministry. If you are bleeding it becomes difficult to help lead others to healing when you need healing yourself. We can be used more effectively when we become healed in our mind, body, and spirit. Although this is Ivy's story and her journey to wholeness, you have your own journey to travel as well. Just know that you are a diamond in the rough just waiting on God to reveal you to the world where you will bring value to whatever life you will touch. Know your worth, you are priceless!

About the Author

Sonja Smith Williams, who is known to so many as First Lady Williams is so much more than you could imagine. Yes, she is a diamond that has been hiding in plain sight but has come forth through ashes and emerged as the leader and dynamic motivator and encourager to so many lives that she has touched. Whether she has touched your life professionally through her profession as a nurse or as a First Lady in ministry or if she has simply crossed your path with her words or her smile, she has truly made an impact in this world. Her heart is poured out constantly to those who connect with her through her ministry Wonderfully Made Me and through her intercessory prayer where she goes to the throne of God on behalf of others. Lady Sonja Williams is the President of Women of Destiny at New Bethel Church of God in Christ in Charlotte, NC where she works hard to encourage and empower women of all ages to be what God wants them to be. She is a wife to Pastor Dennis Williams for 28 years now, mother of 3(Xavier, Rayven, and Jonathan), and a Gigi to Mason, Karson, and Aaliyah. This woman of God longs for those that she encounters to become healthy, healed, and whole. This diamond will continue to shine and stand up for Christ and do what he has called her to do. She is fearfully and wonderfully made as God's masterpiece.

Made in the USA
Columbia, SC
22 March 2024

33475897R00071